Weather

Contents

What is good weather?

Most of us like hot, sunny weather. But different people have different ideas about what is good weather.

My dad's a farmer. He likes rainy weather in the spring.

I don't like it when it's hot weather at school.

I like rainy weather. I enjoy walking in the rain.

I love it when it's hot and sunny on holiday.

What sort of weather do you like? Why?
Do you always like it when it's sunny and warm?
Do you like it when it's raining?

Good and bad weather

Farmers want rain in spring and early summer when the crops are growing. For them, wet weather can be good weather. But they want warm, dry weather at harvest time.

People who like skiing want cold weather with snow. But cold weather can be dangerous too. Snow can block roads and make travelling difficult. For some people, snowy weather is good weather. For others, it is bad weather.

Problems start if the weather does not do what we expect it to. If a winter is colder and snowier than usual, we may not be able to keep roads open. If a summer is too wet, the crops may not get ripe. If it is too dry, the crops may die. We need to know what the weather will be like so that we can plan ahead.

Forecasting the weather

Making a **weather forecast** in our country is difficult. There are many ways of forecasting the weather. Here are some which people have used for a long time.

Weather rhymes

This is a very well-known rhyme:

**Red sky at night,
Shepherd's delight;
Red sky in the morning,
Shepherd's warning.**

In other words, a red sky at night means the next day will be fine, but a red morning sky means rain is coming. Another rhyme goes:

**Rain before seven,
Fine before eleven.**

A farmer working at sunrise

Try testing these two rhymes to see if they are true. Do you know any other rhymes or sayings about the weather?

Weather sayings

There are other sayings which are supposed to tell us what the weather will be like weeks or months ahead. Some people say that if there are a lot of berries on trees and bushes in autumn, the winter will be very cold. But in fact, all this means is that there was a good summer and the trees and bushes were able to make plenty of berries.

Rowan berries

Some people say they can smell rain when it is on its way. Some say that if their bones ache, there will be rain. Others say that if the cows in a field are lying down, there will be rain.

Seaweed is sometimes used to help forecast the weather. There is a saying that the seaweed will be limp and damp if rain is on its way. It will be dry and brittle if the weather is going to be fine.

Looking at clouds

Different kinds of clouds mean different kinds of weather.

Clouds that look like this are a sign of good weather. ⬇

But clouds that look like this mean thunder and rain. ⬇

These clouds mean that rain is on its way.

Some people say that if there is a halo around the moon, rain is on the way. This happens when there is a very fine cloud covering the sky. The saying is usually right.

Choose two ways of forecasting the weather. Do they work? Do you know of any other ways?

Wet playtime!

Is your school ever like this?

How do you decide if it's a wet playtime or not? Can you invent something which lets you know if it's raining enough for it to be a wet playtime or not?

Modern weather forecasting

Some people need to know what the weather will be like for their work. Farmers need to know when it is the right time to gather in their crops. Crops can be harmed by bad weather.

Your school needs to know when it will be good weather for the fête or sports day. Scientists called **meteorologists** try to forecast the weather accurately. Their weather forecasts help farmers. We see the weather forecasters on television.

To make a forecast, a weather forecaster needs information about the air around us. This information is gathered using scientific instruments. Here are some of these instruments:

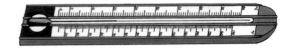

A **thermometer** measures the temperature of the air.

An **anemometer** measures the speed of the wind.

A **weather vane** shows the direction of the wind.

Weather stations and computers

Meteorologists study measurements taken at weather stations all over the country and on ships at sea. They send balloons to carry instruments high above the earth. They collect information from all these instruments and put it into computers. These can build up a picture of how the weather is behaving. The meteorologists use this information to predict the weather.

Weather satellite

Satellites

There are satellites out in space, orbiting the earth. They carry instruments to record temperatures on earth and information about the wind. Satellites send us pictures of the earth's surface, and of the clouds and weather. Meteorologists use information from these photographs to help them predict the weather.

Weather balloon

Can you predict the weather? Do you think the weather will be the same tomorrow as today?

Can you think of other people who need to have accurate weather forecasts?

Shower

fierce

   spring

     rain

       full

drab   gushing

  steely   drain

    sky   grey

      umbrellas   puddled

cars   held   street

  make   high   wellies

   spray   children   for

    birds   want   feet

rain   huddle   out

  becomes   away   harassed

   drops   cats   mothers

    slows   lie   shout

     and   asleep

      stops   plants

      doors   drink

       open   deep

      wide

       people

        step

         outside

Moira Andrew

Thunder and Lightning

Blood punches through every vein
As lightning strips the windowpane.

Under its flashing whip, a white
Village leaps to light.

On tubs of thunder, fists of rain
Slog it out of sight again.

Blood punches the heart with fright
As rain belts the village night.

James Kirkup

Storms

My mum hates thunder
She plugs her ears with a towel
And lies on the settee
As though someone were coming to get her.

But me, I'm alright
I don't mind a bit
I'm a bit edgy about lightning
But thunder doesn't bother me at all.

Glynis Burr

Weather problems

The weather sometimes causes serious problems. For example, in Britain we do not expect very cold weather. But the winter of 1963 was much colder than usual. Roads were blocked with snow and ice. Water pipes froze under the ground because they had not been buried deep enough.

Road blocked with snow

Flooded streets

Floods can also do huge amounts of damage. Floods can wash away crops and farm animals. Homes and belongings can be damaged.

In many countries, people need the rain to fall at the right time of year to water the crops. If it does not come, there is a **drought**. Crops die in the fields. People have nothing to eat. This happened in Africa, in Ethiopia in 1985.

Wind can be dangerous. Strong winds can blow down trees and tear the roofs from homes.

The strongest winds are called **hurricanes**. They are winds that blow very fast. It is unusual for there to be hurricanes in Britain. But in October 1987 there was a hurricane in the south of England. Millions of trees were blown down and many homes were damaged.

Hurricane damage

Photograph of a hurricane taken by a weather satellite

If a weather satellite shows a hurricane is coming, people may be warned to leave their homes and go somewhere safer. If they cannot leave their homes, they must stay indoors with all the windows and doors shut. It is too dangerous to go outside.

The weather forecasters do not always get it right. In October 1987 they did not forecast the hurricane. Everyone was taken by surprise.

Measuring the wind

Is it windy today? How windy is it? If you ask people what they mean by 'breeze' or 'storm', each person will tell you something different.

An officer in the British navy, Admiral Beaufort, thought about this problem. He wrote down what happened when the wind began to blow. He worked out a scale of measurements that everybody could use. It showed clearly what each kind of wind is like. We still use Admiral Beaufort's scale today.

THE BEAUFORT SCALE

Wind strength 0:

CALM
No wind. Chimney-smoke rises straight in the air.

Wind strength 1:

LIGHT AIR
Chimney-smoke drifts gently.

Wind strength 2:

LIGHT BREEZE
You can feel the wind softly stroking your face like a feather.

Wind strength 3:

GENTLE BREEZE
Leaves and twigs move gently on the trees.

Wind strength 4:

MODERATE BREEZE
Dust and rubbish blow about on the ground.

Wind strength 5:

FRESH BREEZE
Small trees bend in the wind.

Wind strength 6:

STRONG BREEZE
Large tree-branches toss and creak. Washing flaps on the line.

Wind strength 7:

NEAR GALE
Whole trees, even the trunks, bend in the wind. Washing is blown from the line.

Wind strength 8:

GALE
Twigs are blown from trees. Crops are flattened in the fields.

Wind strength 9:

STRONG GALE

Large branches snap from trees. Slates and tiles are blown from roofs. Children find it hard to stand against the wind.

Wind strength 10:

STORM

Whole trees are uprooted. Even strong people are blown over.

Wind strength 11:

VIOLENT STORM

Sheds and greenhouses are blown down. Bricks are torn from houses. Chimneys collapse.

Wind strength 12:

HURRICANE

Houses are blown down. Vehicles are hurled about as if by an invisible giant.

Weather wonders

Volcanoes

In 1883 there was one of the biggest explosions there has ever been. Krakatoa, a huge volcano in Indonesia, erupted. Huge amounts of dust and stones and rocks from deep inside the earth were thrown high into the air. This had effects all over the world. Dust fell in the streets of Spain on the other side of the world. And there were cold, wet summers in Europe for two years afterwards.

An active volcano near Krakatoa. The hillside is covered with ash

Mount St Helens volcano in America

Frog rain

Sometimes, the wind blows over a pond and carries tiny frogs into the air. The frogs can be blown for hundreds of miles. When they fall to the earth, it looks like it is raining frogs!

Hail lying in a field of damaged crops

Hail

Hail is caused by the moisture in clouds freezing and falling to earth as ice. Hail can damage crops in the fields. Hailstones are usually quite small. But in 1970, one fell in America that weighed three quarters of a kilogram. It was as big as a melon!

Snow

Have you ever looked at a snowflake through a magnifying glass? It is easiest to do it outside so the snow doesn't melt too quickly. All snowflakes have six sides like a hexagon, or six points like a star. And all snowflakes are different – no two are the same. They are very beautiful.

Snow crystal

Climates

When we talk about the kind of weather a country has, we talk about its **climate**.

Cold climates

In countries like Austria, where there is a lot of snow every winter, everyone is prepared for the winter weather. The houses have to be warm and well heated. They often have steep roofs to help the snow slide off them easily.

Snow ploughs keep the roads clear of snow. In the coldest places, there are special sledges with motors for travelling about on the snow.

Snow plough

Snow sledge

Hot climates

In countries where the weather can be hot, houses often have shutters over the windows to help keep the heat out. Fans or air-conditioning keep the rooms cool.

Wet seasons and dry seasons

The warmer parts of the world often have a rainy season and dry season. Farmers plant their crops when the rains fall. They harvest them when the weather is dry and the crops are ripe. The rains are very important to them.

Farming in the rain in Bangladesh

Wet climates

In wet countries, people often build their homes on high ground, out of the way of rivers. If the rivers flood, their homes are safe.

Glossary

anemometer
An instrument which measures the speed of the wind.

climate
The kind of weather a country has.

drought
A period when rain is expected but does not fall. During a drought, plants die because of lack of water. That means there is very little for animals or people to eat.

hurricane
Extremely strong winds.

meteorologist
A scientist who uses scientific information to make weather forecasts.

thermometer
An instrument which measures temperature.

weather forecast
A prediction of what will happen to the weather, if it will stay the same or how it will change. Weather forecasts are made for the next 24 hours, or for a longer period.

weather vane
An instrument which measures the direction of the wind.